AAT

Internal Accounting Systems and Controls

Pocket Notes

These Pocket Notes support study for the following AAT qualifications:
AAT Diploma in Professional Accounting – Level 4
AAT Diploma in Business Skills – Level 4
AAT Diploma in Professional Accounting at SCQF Level 8

British library cataloguing-in-publication data

A catalogue record for this book is available from the British Library.

Published by:
Kaplan Publishing UK
Unit 2 The Business Centre
Molly Millars Lane
Wokingham
Berkshire
RG41 2QZ

ISBN 978-1-83996-082-6

© Kaplan Financial Limited, 2021

Printed and bound in Great Britain.

This Product includes content from the International Ethics Standards Board for Accountants (IESBA), published by the International Federation of Accountants (IFAC) in 2015 and is used with permission of IFAC.

The text in this material and any others made available by any Kaplan Group company does not amount to advice on a particular matter and should not be taken as such. No reliance should be placed on the content as the basis for any investment or other decision or in connection with any advice given to third parties. Please consult your appropriate professional adviser as necessary. Kaplan Publishing Limited and all other Kaplan group companies expressly disclaim all liability to any person in respect of any losses or other claims, whether direct, indirect, incidental, consequential or otherwise arising in relation to the use of such materials.

Contents

Preface

These Pocket Notes contain the key things that you need to know for the exam, presented in a unique visual way that makes revision easy and effective.

Written by experienced lecturers and authors, these Pocket Notes break down content into manageable chunks to maximise your concentration.

Quality and accuracy are of the utmost importance to us so if you spot an error in any of our products, please send an email to mykaplanreporting@kaplan.com with full details, or follow the link to the feedback form in MyKaplan.

Our Quality Co-ordinator will work with our technical team to verify the error and take action to ensure it is corrected in future editions.

A guide to the assessment

The assessment

The Internal Accounting Systems and Controls (INAC) Assessment is assessed by means of a computer based assessment. The CBA will last for 2½ hours.

In any one assessment, students may not be assessed on all content, or on the full depth or breadth of a piece of content. The content assessed may change over time to ensure validity of assessment, but all assessment criteria will be tested over time.

Learning outcomes & weighting

Assessment objective	Weighting
1 Understand the role and responsibilities of the accounting function within an organisation	10%
2 Evaluate internal control systems	25%
3 Evaluate an organisation's accounting system and underpinning procedures	25%
4 Understand the impact of technology on accounting systems	15%
5 Recommend improvements to an organisation's accounting system	25%
Total	**100%**

Pass mark

To pass the assessment, students need to achieve a mark of 70% or more.

This unit contributes 20% of the total amount required for the Diploma in Professional Accounting qualification.

1

The accounting function

- Organisations and the need for control.
- The accounting function.
- Relationships with other departments.
- Coordination between accounting and other business functions.
- Understanding systems.
- Regulation and legislation.

Organisations and the need for control

Definition

'Organisations are social arrangements for the controlled performance of collective goals'.

Control mechanisms

Methods of control
Organisational structure
Target setting and budgeting
Direct supervision
Culture
Self-control
Control Systems – e.g. actual v budget
Control processes – e.g. control account reconciliations

Organisational Structure

How to discuss structure
The division of responsibility
The degree of decentralisation
The length of the scalar chain
The size of the span of control
Whether organisations are 'tall' or 'flat'

The accounting function

The role of the accounting function

There are four components to the function

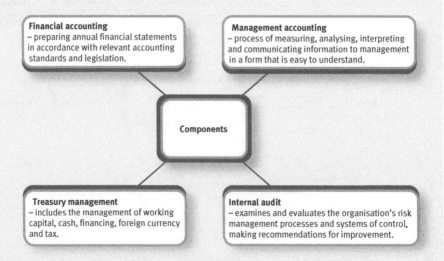

Financial accounting
– preparing annual financial statements in accordance with relevant accounting standards and legislation.

Management accounting
– process of measuring, analysing, interpreting and communicating information to management in a form that is easy to understand.

Components

Treasury management
– includes the management of working capital, cash, financing, foreign currency and tax.

Internal audit
– examines and evaluates the organisation's risk management processes and systems of control, making recommendations for improvement.

Relationships with other departments

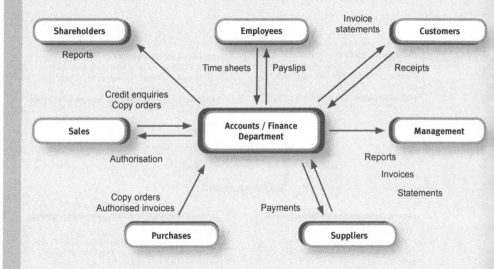

Coordination between accounting and other business functions

Department	Areas of interaction
Purchasing	Establishing credit terms Monitoring payments Inventory and cost control
Production	Cost measurements and overhead allocation Budgeting (e.g. units, quantity) Achieving efficiency and economy
HR	Recruitment and training expenditure Salary payment, estimating PAYE liabilities Reward plans, tax-efficient benefits packages
IT	Systems design and development Improving access to information Incorporating new technology into operations
Customer services	Pricing additional services (e.g. maintenance) Assessing costs of product failures Qualitative feedback on operations
Marketing	Advertising budgets Product pricing Estimating market share

Understanding systems

General systems

Example – If we are concentrating on the finance system, then sales, production and purchasing become part of the environment, and within the system boundary will be found smaller subsystems such as product costing, financial accounting and treasury.

Control systems

- **Standard** – is what the system is aiming for.
- **Sensor** (or detector) – measures the output of the system.
- **Comparator** – compares the information from the standard and the sensor.
- **Effector** (or activator) – initiates the control action.
- **Feedback** – is the information that is taken from the system output and used to adjust the system.

Regulation and legislation

Responsibility to regulatory authorities:

- Companies House (e.g. submission of financial statement for inspection by interested parties).
- Tax authorities (e.g. HMRC for VAT, PAYE, corporation tax).
- Financial services (e.g. stock exchange for listed companies).
- Regulators, where appropriate (e.g. Charities Commission, Ofcom).

Companies Act 2006 sets out that financial statements have to give a "true and fair view".

IFRS Foundation supervises the development of international standards and guidance. It's a parent entity of:

- International Accounting Standards Board (IASB): aims to develop a single set of quality, understandable and enforceable accounting standards.
- FRS Interpretation Committee (IFRS IC): reviews widespread accounting issues and provides guidance.
- IFRS Advisory Council (IFRS AC): consults the users of financial information and offers advice to the IFRS Foundation.

2

Financial information and stakeholders

- Purpose of financial statements.
- Purpose of management reports.
- Stakeholders.

Purpose of financial statements

Purpose of financial statements

The statement of financial position	Provides information on the financial position of a business (its assets and liabilities at a point in time).
The statement of profit or loss	Provides information on the performance of a business (the profit or loss which results from trading over a period of time).
The statement of other comprehensive income	Shows income and expenses that are not recognised in profit or loss.
The statement of changes in equity	Provides information about how the equity of the company has changed over the period.
The statement of cash flow	Provides information on the financial adaptability of a business (the movement of cash into and out of the business over a period of time).

Stewardship

Stewardship is the accountability of management for the resources entrusted to it by the owners or the Government.

Purpose of management reports

Needs of management

Planning	Planning involves establishing the objectives of an organisation and formulating relevant strategies that can be used to achieve those objectives.
Decision making	In most situations, decision making involves making a choice between two or more alternatives.
Control	Output from operations is measured and reported ('fed back') to management, and actual results are compared against the plan in control reports.
	Managers take corrective action where appropriate, especially in the case of exceptionally bad or good performance.

Key reports

- Budget reports, detailing budgetary plans for future periods.
- Variance reports comparing actual and budget performance, to facilitate effective control.
- Reports of key performance indicators to ensure that management focus on what is important to the success of the organisation.
- One-off reports that look at individual decisions.

Evaluating a management report – factors to consider

- The basis of preparation
- The methods used
- The figures used
- The impact on people concerned

Stakeholders

Needs of stakeholders

Internal	
Shareholders	Need to identify how management use funds and assess ability of business to pay dividends.
Management	Need information with which to assess performance, take decisions, plan, and control the business.
Employees and their unions	Need information to help them negotiate pay and benefits.
External	
Investors	Need to be able to assess the ability of a business to pay dividends and manage resources.
Customers	Need to be assured that their supply will continue into the future.
Suppliers	Need to be assured that they will continue to get paid and on time and the financial statements will help with this.
Lenders, such as banks	Interested in the ability of the business to pay interest and repay loans.
HM Revenue and Customs	Uses financial statements as the basis for tax assessments.
The public (especially pressure groups)	Will look at the financial reports and statements to aid their understanding of profits an organisation may be making from activities to which the pressure group are opposed.

3

Internal control systems

- Internal control.
- Typical control activities (SPAMSOAP).
- Internal audit.
- Sales system.
- Purchases system.
- Payroll system.
- Inventory system.
- Bank and cash system.
- Effect of weaknesses.
- Segregation of duties revisited.

Internal control

Internal control consists of the following components (ISA 315):

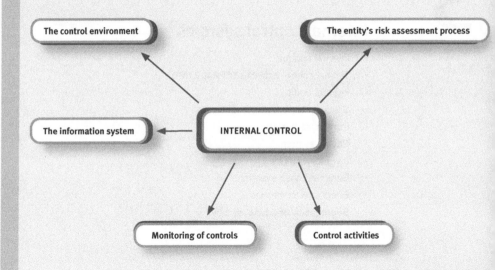

Typical control activities (SPAMSOAP)

Segregation of duties	Keep separate the custodial function, the authorisation function, the recording function and the execution function.
Physical controls	Access to assets and records is only permitted to authorised personnel.
Authorisation and approval	All transactions require authorisation or approval by a responsible person.
Management	Controls exercised by the management outside the day-to-day routine of the system.
Supervision	Supervisory procedures by the management.
Organisation	A well-defined organisational structure showing how responsibility and authority are delegated.
Arithmetical and accounting	E.g. control accounts, cross totals, reconciliations and sequential controls over documents.
Personnel	Well-motivated, competent personnel who possess the necessary integrity for their tasks.

Internal audit

Definition

'an independent, objective assurance and consulting activity designed to add value and improve an organisation's operations.'

What do internal auditors do?

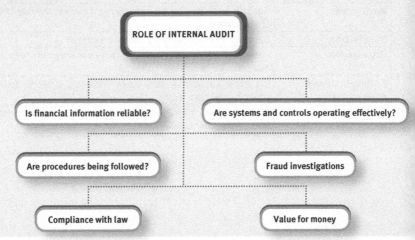

Sales system

Stage 1 — Order received

Stage 2 — Goods despatched

Stage 3 — Invoice sent

Stage 4 — Transactions recorded in books

Stage 5 — Cash received

Control objectives

The objectives of controls in the sales system are to ensure that:

- goods are only supplied to customers who pay promptly and in full
- orders are despatched promptly and in full to the correct customer
- only valid sales are recorded
- all sales and related receivables are recorded
- revenue is recorded in the period to which it relates
- sales are recorded accurately and related receivables are recorded at an appropriate value.

Purchases system

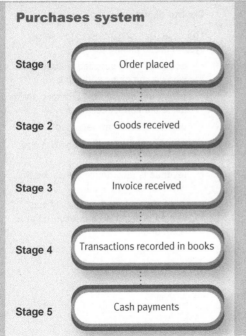

Stage 1	Order placed
Stage 2	Goods received
Stage 3	Invoice received
Stage 4	Transactions recorded in books
Stage 5	Cash payments

Control objectives

The objectives of controls in the purchase system are to ensure that:

- all purchases are of the appropriate quality and price
- only necessary goods/services are procured
- all purchases and related payables are recorded
- expenditure is recorded in the period to which it relates
- expenditure is recorded accurately and related payables are recorded at an appropriate value.

Payroll system

Stage 1 — Clock cards submitted and input

Stage 2 — Gross pay, deductions and net pay calculated

Stage 3 — Other amendments input

Stage 4 — Final payroll calculated and payslips produced

Stage 5 — Payments to employees and tax authorities

Stage 6 — Payroll costs and payments recorded

Control objectives

The objectives of controls in the payroll system are to ensure that:

- only genuine employees are paid
- employees are only paid for work done
- employees are paid at the correct rates of pay
- gross pay is calculated and recorded accurately
- net pay is calculated and recorded accurately; and
- correct amounts owed are recorded and paid to the taxation authorities.

Inventory system

Control objectives — Control procedures

Inventory system

Goods received — Goods despatched

Receipt recorded — Despatch recorded

Inventory movement recorded

Control objectives

The objectives of controls in the inventory system are to ensure that:

- inventory levels meet the needs of production (raw materials and components) and customer demand (finished goods)

- inventory levels are not excessive, preventing obsolescence and unnecessary storage costs

- inventory is safeguarded from theft, loss or damage

- all inventory received and despatched is correctly recorded on a timely basis at the appropriate value

- only inventory owned by the company is recorded.

Bank and cash system

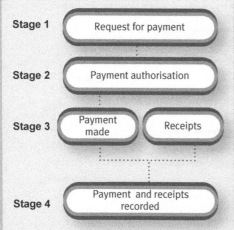

Stage 1 — Request for payment

Stage 2 — Payment authorisation

Stage 3 — Payment made | Receipts

Stage 4 — Payment and receipts recorded

Control objectives

The objectives of controls in the cash cycle are to ensure that:

- petty cash levels are kept to a minimum, preventing theft
- payments can only be made for legitimate business expenditure
- cash and chequebooks are safeguarded
- receipts are banked on a timely basis
- cash movements are recorded on a timely basis.

Effect of weaknesses

Control weaknesses might have effects on a number of areas. Make sure that you consider the full impact.

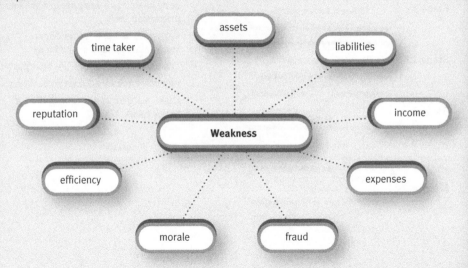

Segregation of duties revisited

Purchases	The persons who raise purchase orders should be independent of the ledger keeping function, the stock recording and control subsystem and the cheque.
Sales	The persons responsible for preparation of sales orders should be independent of credit control, custody of stock and recording sales transactions.
	The credit controller should be independent of the sales order clerks.
	The warehouse/despatch department should be independent of sales order preparation, credit control and invoicing.
	Sales invoicing should be independent of sales order preparation, credit control, warehouse and despatch departments.
	The sales ledger clerk should be independent of sales order preparation, credit control, warehouse, despatch and sales invoicing.
	The sales ledger control account should be maintained independent of the sales ledger clerk.
Cash	The persons who sign the cheques should be different from those who handle the authorisation of purchase invoices.
	The persons who are responsible for opening the post, preparing the paying-in details and controlling the sales ledger should be separate functionaries.

4

Internal controls in a computerised environment

- Information systems controls.
- Data security.
- Integrity controls.
- Controls.
- Systems integrity in a network environment.
- Assessing and managing risk.
- Contingency controls.

Information systems controls

General controls

General controls relate to the environment within which computer-based systems are developed, maintained and operated and are generally applicable to all the applications running on the system.

Training programmes	To ensure competence and reduce errors.
Authorisation procedures for program amendments and testing	To prevent unwanted changes being made.
Physical security of hardware and software	To prevent accidental or malicious damage or natural disasters.
Back-up procedures (maintaining copies of files off-site, back-up facilities).	To ensure data and systems can be recovered.
Access controls.	e.g. firewalls and anti-virus checkers.
Segregation of duties	To minimise tampering with programs or data.
Hacking prevention measures	To ensure the system is not accessed during data transmission (hacking).
Efficiency measures	Controls to ensure that the computing resources are used efficiently.
Recruitment policies	To ensure honesty and competence.

Data security

Data security measures involve different aspects:

- **Physical security**, such as the security of data storage facilities, from flood as well as unauthorised access
- **Software security**, such as maintaining a log of all failed access requests, and
- **Operational security**, with regard to such things as work data being taken home by employees, and periodic data protection audits of the computer systems.

Physical Security controls

Fire systems and procedures	e.g. fire alarms, heat and smoke detectors.
Location of hardware	e.g. away from risk of flooding.
Regular building maintenance	e.g. attention to roofs, windows and doors will reduce the risk of water penetration and make forcible entry more difficult.
Physical access controls	e.g. security guards to check identification and authorisation, CCTV, using badge readers or coded locks on access doors from public areas and electronic tagging of hardware.

Individual staff controls

Logical access system	e.g. identification of the user, authentication of user identity and checks on user authority.
Personal identification	e.g. PIN, fingerprint recognition, eye retina 'prints' and voice 'prints'.
Storage of CDs, removable data storage devices in secure locations	e.g. back-up data is stored in a fire-proof environment on-site, and occasionally some form of master back-up is removed from the installation site completely.

Integrity controls

Activities

Data integrity means completeness and accuracy of data.

For decisions to be made consistently throughout the organisation, it is necessary for the system to contain controls over the input, processing and output of data to maintain its integrity.

Input activities	File processing activities	Output activities
• data collection and preparation • data authorisation • data conversion (if appropriate) • data transmission • data correction • corrected data re-input	• data validation and edit • data manipulation, sorting/ merging • master file updating	• output control and reconciliation with predetermined data • information distribution

Controls

Input Controls	Validation controls
• Verification	• Comparison of totals
• Type checks	• Comparison of data sets
• Non-existence checks	• Sequence numbers
• Consistency checks	• Range checks
• Duplication checks	• Format checks
• Range checks	
• Input comparisons	
• Batch and hash totals	
• One-for-one checks	

Processing controls	Output controls
• Standardisation	• Batch control totals
• Batch control	• Start or report / page number / end of report markers
• Double processing	• Distribution lists

Systems integrity in a network environment

Risks

- Hardware/software disruption or malfunction
- Computer viruses
- Unauthorised access to the system

Controls

- Physical access controls
- User identification
- Data and program access authorisation
- Program integrity controls
- Database integrity controls
- Anti-virus software
- Surveillance
- Communication lines safeguards
- Encryption
- Firewalls

Assessing and managing risk

Types of risk

- disasters outside the control of the organisation
- poor trading
- mismanagement
- errors due to human or machine problems
- misappropriation of resources and assets

Risk assessment process

- Identify risks.
- Quantify risks.
- Identify counter measures.
- Cost counter measures.
- Choose which counter measures are required.
- Draw up contingency plans.
- Implement the plan to manage the risk.
- Monitor, review and update the plan.
- Constantly watch for new risks.

Counter measures

- Transfer risks by means of an insurance policy.
- Accept risks if counter measures cannot be justified.
- Modify system to eliminate risks.
- Reduce probability of risk by introducing controls.
- Reduce exposure to risk by removing organisation from risky situations.
- Adopt measures to reduce cost associated with a risk.
- Enable recovery by implementing recovery procedures.

Contingency controls

Disasters

In computing terms, a disaster might mean the loss or unavailability of some of the computer systems.

Contingency Plan

- Standby procedures – so that essential operations can be performed while normal services are disrupted.
- Recovery procedures – to return to normal working once the breakdown is fixed.
- Management policies – to ensure that the plan is implemented.

- Controls
- Distributed support, where computing is spread over several sites.
- Reciprocal agreement with another company.
- A commercial computer bureau.
- Empty rooms / equipped rooms.
- Relocatable computer centres.

5

Information and technology

- Data and information.
- Information systems.
- Cloud accounting.
- Artificial Intelligence (AI).
- Big Data and analytics.
- Cyber security.

Data and information

Data consists of numbers, letters, symbols, raw facts, events and transactions, which have been recorded but not yet processed into a form that is suitable for making decisions.

Information is data that has been processed in such a way that it has meaning to the person that receives it, who may then use it to improve the quality of their decision-making.

Good information should have the following characteristics (ACCURATE).

Accurate

Complete

Cost-effective

Understandable

Relevant

Adaptable

Timely

Easy to use

Information systems

Information technology (IT) describes any equipment concerned with the capture, storage, transmission or presentation of data.

Put simply, IT is the hardware infrastructure that runs the information systems. This will include desktops, laptops, servers, printers and hard drives used by the organisation.

Information systems (IS) refer to the management and provision of information to support the running of the organisation.

Levels of management

There are three levels of management: strategic, tactical and operational, requiring different types of information.

Strategic requires information from internal and external sources in order to plan the long-term strategies of the organisation.

Tactical requires information and instructions from the strategic level of management, together with routine and regular quantitative information from the operational level of management.

Operational requires information and instructions from the tactical level of management, and is primarily concerned with the day-to-day performance of tasks and most of the information is obtained from internal sources.

Types of information system

Transaction processing system (TPS)

Records all daily transactions of the organisation, summarised and reported on a routine basis.

Transaction processing systems are used mainly by operational managers to make basic decisions.

Management information systems (MIS)

Converts data from TPS into information for tactical managers, designed to help them monitor performance, maintain co-ordination and provide background information about the organisation's operations.

Executive information systems (EIS)

Provides strategic managers with flexible access to information from the entire business, as well as relevant information from the external environment.

Enables senior management to easily model the entire business by turning its data into useful, summarised reports.

Information dashboards

EIS reports are often presented as 'dashboards', combining multiple pieces of useful information onto a single screen or page, in the same way that the dashboard on a car presents the driver with all the information necessary to drive the car.

This enables senior management to focus on key areas.

Cloud accounting

Cloud computing is computing based on the internet, avoiding the need for physical computer storage, allowing users to log in and perform accounting functions on any computer with an internet connection.

Benefits of cloud accounting

Storing and sharing data – usually able to store more data than local physical drives, data can be shared more easily.

On-demand self-service – users can gain access to technology on demand.

Flexibility – no need to be plugged into networks to access data needed.

Collaboration – better collaboration as documents can be worked on simultaneously by many different users.

More competitive – allows small organisations to compete with larger rivals.

Easier scaling – the service can grow with the business, providing flexibility in terms of size, authorised users etc.

Reduced maintenance – cloud takes care of regular maintenance and system updates.

Back-ups – removes need for physical devices to store backed-up data, adding security.

Disaster recovery – improved back-up procedures aid disaster recovery.

Better security – reduced risks of loss or damage of hardware.

Disadvantages of cloud accounting

Reliance on cloud service provider – if service provider's servers go down for any reason user's business is halted until service is resumed.

Regulatory risks – user needs to ensure that service provider acts responsibly and follows all relevant regulations.

Unauthorised access to data – service provider staff could access user's data without authorisation.

Artificial Intelligence (AI)

Artificial Intelligence: area of computer science, emphasising creation of intelligent machines to work and react like human beings.

Machine learning

Machine learning algorithms:

- detect patterns

- make predictions and recommendations by processing data and experiences, rather than by explicit programming instruction

- adapt to new data and experiences to improve their function over time.

Artificial intelligence and accountancy

Short to medium term

AI will enable accountants to

- improve their efficiency by doing routine tasks more quickly and reliably

- provide more insight if useful information is produced

- deliver more value to businesses.

Longer term

Systems will increasingly carry out decision-making tasks currently performed by humans, bringing opportunities for much more radical change, including:

- using machine-learning to code accounting entries, improving accuracy and enabling greater process automation

- improving fraud detection through more sophisticated, machine-learning models of 'normal' activities and better prediction of fraudulent activities

- using machine-learning-based predictive models to forecast revenues

- improving analysis of unstructured data, such as contracts and emails.

Big Data and analytics

Big Data is a term for a collection of data so large that it becomes difficult to deal with using traditional processing.

Examples of Big Data

- social network traffic
- web server logs
- streamed audio content
- banking transactions
- web page histories and content
- government documentation
- financial market data

Features of Big Data

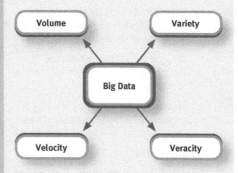

Volume – amount of data the organisation needs to store and process.

Variety – numerous sources from which data is received.

Velocity – speed at which data changes.

Veracity – data gathered needs to be accurate, otherwise it's meaningless.

Benefits of Big Data

- Driving innovation by reducing time taken to answer key business questions, speeding up decision process.

- Gaining competitive advantage by identifying trends or information not yet identified by rivals.

- Improving productivity by identifying waste and inefficiency, or identifying improvements to working procedures.

Data analytics

Descriptive analytics looks at past data statistically to help a business understand how it has performed. It can help stakeholders interpret information, perhaps with data visualisations like graphs, charts, reports, and dashboards, enabling non-financial managers to interpret information.

Diagnostic analytics takes descriptive data and provides deeper analysis to help understand why things happened.

Predictive analytics takes historical data and feeds it into a machine-learning model, considering key trends and patterns, then applying this model to current data to predict what will happen next.

Prescriptive analytics uses predictive data to suggest various courses of action, outlining potential implications for each.

Data visualisation

Data visualisation is used to make data relevant, accessible and easy for all end-users, especially non-financial users.

Key benefits

Accessibility – data visualisation graphics and dashboards are designed to be more user-friendly than traditional financial reports, which can be difficult to understand and visually unappealing.

Real-time synchronising – real-time data with data visualisation tools gives up-to-date, clear, information, allowing quicker responses to business changes.

Performance optimisation – better decision-making is supported by clear, timely information, enabling proactive utilisation of resources as problems are identified.

Insight and understanding – Visual presentation of data leads to improved understanding of cause and effect relationships underpinning performance.

Cyber security

Cyber security: protection of internet-connected systems, including hardware, software and data, from cyber-attacks.

Cyber-attack: malicious, deliberate attempt to breach information system of another individual or organisation. Attacker usually seeks some benefit from disrupting victim's network.

Cyber-attacks may include:

Malware – short for malicious software, designed to cause damage, rendering computer or network inoperable, or granting the attacker access to control the system remotely.

Phishing – cyber criminals craft emails to fool a target into taking harmful action, such as clicking on a disguised link that downloads malware, or takes them to a fake website where they will be asked for sensitive information such as usernames and passwords.

Denial of service attacks – a brute force method preventing an online service from working properly. For example, attackers might flood a website with so much traffic that it overwhelms the system's ability to function.

Man-in-the-middle attacks – attackers secretly interpose themselves between the user and a web service that the user is trying to access. For example, an attacker might set up a Wi-Fi network with a login screen designed to mimic a hotel network. When a user logs in, the attacker harvests any information that user sends, including passwords.

6

Preventing and detecting fraud

- What is fraud?
- Fraud risk management.
- Types of fraud.
- Implications of fraud.
- Fraud detection.
- Fraud response.
- Risk management.
- Risk matrices.
- Fraud matrix.

What is fraud?

Definitions

- Dishonestly obtaining an advantage, avoiding an obligation or causing a loss to another party.
- Note: distinction made between fraud and errors (unintentional mistakes).

Examples of fraud

Crimes against customers	e.g. pyramid schemes; selling counterfeit goods
Employee fraud against employers	e.g. falsifying expense claims
Crimes against investors, consumers and employees	e.g. falsifying financial statements
Crimes against financial institutions	e.g. fraudulent insurance claims
Crimes against government	e.g. social security benefit claims fraud; tax evasion
Crimes by professional criminals	e.g. money laundering
E-crime by people using computers	e.g. spamming; copyright crimes; hacking

Fraud risk management

Prerequisites for fraud

- An ability to rationalise the fraudulent action and hence act with dishonesty.
- A perceived opportunity to commit fraud.
- A motive, incentive or pressure to commit fraud.

Fraud prevention

- Anti-fraud culture
- Risk awareness
- Whistleblowing
- Sound internal control systems

Fraud deterrence

Only when potential fraudsters believe fraud will be detected and when whistle-blowers believe they will be protected will there be an effective deterrence of fraud.

Types of fraud

- theft
- false accounting
- collusion
- computer fraud

Implications of fraud

Any fraud discovered

- Negative publicity
- Suppliers withdraw credit?
- Customers look elsewhere?
- Fraudsters arrested

Theft of funds or assets

- Lower profits
- Reduced working capital

Results artificially enhanced

- Too much profit distributed to shareholders

- Lower retained profits
- Inaccurate information for investors
- Suppliers misled re credit

Results understated

- Loan access restricted
- Share price may fall
- Reduced returns to investors
- Tax investigation

Fraud detection

- Performing regular checks.
- Warning signals/fraud risk indicators.
- Failures in internal control procedures

  - Lack of information provided to auditors

  - Unusual behaviour by individual staff members

  - Accounting difficulties.

- Whistleblowers.

Fraud response

- Response plan:

  - Internal disciplinary action

  - Civil litigation

  - Criminal prosecution

  - Responsibilities clearly set out

Risk management

Risk identification	Risk identification – producing lists of risk items.
Risk analysis	Risk analysis – assessing loss probability and magnitude for each item.
Risk prioritisation	Risk prioritisation – producing a ranked ordering of risk items.
Risk-management planning	Risk-management planning – deciding how to address each risk item.
Risk resolution	Risk resolution – producing a situation in which risk items are eliminated or resolved.
Risk monitoring	Risk monitoring – tracking progress toward resolving risk items and taking corrective action.

Risk matrices

Low, medium, high matrix

		Impact		
		Low (1)	Medium (2)	High (3)
Likelihood/ probability	High (3)	3	6	9
	Medium (2)	2	4	6
	Low (1)	1	2	3

TARA matrix

		Impact	
		Low	High
Likelihood/ probability	High	Reduce	Avoid
	Low	Accept	Transfer

Fraud matrix

Impact

The impact of a fraud can be graded:

- **high** – effects of fraud are very serious for the organisation, affecting its profit and/or liquidity
- **moderate** – effects of fraud are significant but can be dealt with internally, or in some cases by the police
- **low** – impact of fraud is insignificant (petty pilfering)

Format

Matrix format will vary, but the example below is fairly typical.

Details of risk	Employees	Collusion	Likelihood	Impact
Stationery pilferage	Payroll staff	None	high	Low
Theft of cash	Payroll staff	None	moderate	moderate
Payment to fictitious employees	Payroll staff	Third party recipient	moderate	moderate

A simpler fraud matrix simply lists the details of the fraud risk with a numerical value rating the fraud, typically from 1 to 5:

5	Very high
4	High
3	Medium
2	Low
1	Very low

So the payroll department matrix above becomes:

Details of risk	Rating
Stationery pilferage	1
Theft of cash	3
Payment to fictitious employees	3

7

Performance indicators

- Ratio calculations.
- Interpreting ratios.
- Limitations of ratio analysis.
- Linking ratios and control problems.

Ratio calculations

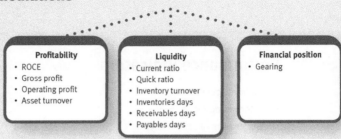

Profitability
- ROCE
- Gross profit
- Operating profit
- Asset turnover

Liquidity
- Current ratio
- Quick ratio
- Inventory turnover
- Inventories days
- Receivables days
- Payables days

Financial position
- Gearing

Profitability

$$ROCE = \frac{PBIT}{Capital\ Employed\ (Equity + Debt)} \times 100\%$$

$$Gross\ profit\ margin = \frac{Gross\ profit}{Revenue} \times 100\%$$

$$Operating\ profit\ margin = \frac{PBIT}{Revenue} \times 100\%$$

$$Asset\ turnover = \frac{Revenue}{Capital\ Employed} \times 100\%$$

Short-term liquidity

Current ratio = $\dfrac{\text{Current Assets}}{\text{Current liabilities}}$:1

Quick ratio = $\dfrac{\text{Current Assets} - \text{Inventory}}{\text{Current liabilities}}$

Efficiency ratios (working capital)

Inventory turnover = $\dfrac{\text{COS}}{\text{Inventories}}$

Inventory days = $\dfrac{\text{Inventories}}{\text{COS}}$ x 365 days

Trade receivables collection
period = $\dfrac{\text{Trade receivables}}{\text{Revenue}}$ x 365 days

Trade payables collection
period = $\dfrac{\text{Trade payables}}{\text{Purchases (or COS)}}$ x 365 days

Long-term solvency

Gearing = $\dfrac{\text{Debt}}{\text{Equity}}$ x 100% or $\dfrac{\text{Debt}}{\text{Debt} + \text{Equity}}$

Interpreting ratios

It is important to understand the meaning of the ratios as well as calculating them for the exam.

- What does the ratio literally mean?
- What does a change in the ratio mean?
- What is the norm?
- What are the limitations of the ratio?

The exam

In the exam you may be asked to:

- identify what is indicated by the ratios
- explain why the ratios are different, from one period to another or between companies
- summarise cause and effect correctly.

When explaining why ratios have changed, always refer to the underlying drivers of business performance.

Limitations of ratio analysis

- Ratios do not provide answers; they merely highlight significant features or trends in the financial statements. They usually highlight areas that need further investigation.
- Be mindful of seasonal trade as accounting year-ends are often just after the seasonal trend is over when the business is at its best.
- Watch out for window dressing in the financial statements such as collecting receivables just before the year-end in order to show a larger cash balance and lower receivables than is normal.
- Accounting ratios are based on accounting information and are only as accurate as that underlying accounting information.
- If comparisons are to be made they must be with companies with a similar trade, otherwise the pattern of ratios will be different and the comparisons meaningless.

Linking ratios and control problems

From problems to ratios – examples

Control issue	Impact on financial statements	Key ratios affected
Fraud where items are stolen from the warehouse	• Cost of sales will higher than expected	• Fall in gross and net margins
Credit controller ill	• Receivables balance will be higher than expected	• Receivables days higher • Quick and current ratios higher
Theft of cash	• Less cash than expected	• Quick and current ratios lower
Fraud where items are sold to a friend at a very low price	• Sales lower than expected • Gross profit lower than expected	• Fall in gross and net margins • Receivables days lower

From ratios to problems – examples

Ratio	Basic causes	Possible control issues
Gross margin down	• Prices lower and / or costs of sales higher	• Sales managers giving excessive discounts • Theft of inventory • Excessive waste / obsolescence of stock • Cut-off problems • Price rises from suppliers unchecked due to purchase orders not being authorised correctly
Inventory days higher	• Excessive period – end inventory • Cost of sales lower	• Purchased too much inventory due to purchase orders not being checked properly • Purchase invoices mis-recorded • Errors with time sheets

8

Changes to the accounting system

- Reasons for change.
- Justification of change.
- Implementing changes – dealing with resistance.
- Implementing changes – approaches.
- Training model.

Reasons for change

Reason for change	Example
Regulation changes	VAT rules change
Growth	Old manual approach cannot cope with growth
New information flow	Government introduces new reporting requirements
Short-term capacity issues	Computer failure requiring temporary manual system
Identified weakness	New levels of authorisation needed
Changes in the environment	Increased focus on environmental factors
New products	Updates to ledger accounts and accounting process

Justification of change

Cost-benefit analysis

Tangible costs	Intangible costs
• One-off costs (e.g. development, buying new equipment) • On-going costs (e.g. maintenance, replaceable items)	• Staff dissatisfaction if systems are poorly specified or implemented. • The cost of increased staff mistakes and reduced performance during the learning period after a new system is implemented. • Opportunity costs. • Lock-in costs. Purchasing a particular solution can bind a company to a particular supplier, reducing its ability to take advantage of future developments from other providers.
Tangible benefits	Intangible benefits
• Savings in staff salaries, maintenance costs and consumables. • Greater efficiency. • Business benefits gained through improved management information. • Gaining competitive advantage.	• More informed or quicker decision-making. • Improved customer service, resulting in increased customer satisfaction. • Freedom from routine decisions and activities, resulting in more time being available for strategic planning and innovation. • Better understanding of customer needs through improved analysis of data.

Techniques

• Payback • NPV • SWOT • PESTLE

Implementing changes – dealing with resistance

Resistance

Job Factors	These generally revolve around fear – fear of new technology, fear of change or fear of demotion or levels of pay.
Social Factors	The people affected may dislike the potential new social dynamic (or like the existing social scene and not want that to change).
Personal factors	These, by definition, are more varied as each person may react differently to a particular change.

Response

Source of resistance	Possible response
• The need for security and the familiar.	• Provide information and encouragement, invite involvement.
• Having the opinion that no change is needed.	• Clarify the purpose of the change and how it will be made.
• Trying to protect vested interests.	• Demonstrate the problem or the opportunity that makes changes desirable.
• Dislike the social upheaval.	• Organise social team building events.

Implementing changes – approaches

Testing

Realistic data testing	The new system is tested against normal transactions to ensure it operates as expected.
Contrived testing	The new system is presented with unusual data to see how it reacts e.g. negative sales invoices.
Volume testing	A common problem with systems is that they fail to cope when volumes increase, so this is tested in advance. Systems may crash or slow down excessively.
User acceptance testing	Systems are often designed by IT experts but then used by people with much less IT skill.

Changeover method

Direct	The old system ceases and the new system takes over on the same day.
Parallel	In this system both the old and new systems are run at the same time.
Pilot	The new system is piloted in a particular location. In this way operational bugs can be identified and removed before wider implementation takes place.
Phased	This is similar to a pilot, but it is the phrase used when the system is introduced in stages or in one sub system at a time.

Training model

Identify training need	Identify skills necessary for the job, skills of the job-holder and extent of gap.
Design, prepare and deliver	Training is tailored to fill the gap, trainee is trained.
Reaction and learning	Review trainee's feelings towards training provided, extent that training content absorbed.
Transfer lesson to job	Use and time of the newly trained personnel should be optimised.
Effect of training	Difficult to accurately assess the effects of training provided, may need to rely on trainee interviews.
Positive behaviour	Important to maintain positive impact of training for as long as possible.

9

Ethics and sustainability

- Ethics.
- Fundamental principles.
- Examples.
- Safeguards.
- Sustainability.
- Benefits of acting sustainably.
- Sustainability and the accounting system.

Ethics

What is ethics?

- Morality – the difference between right and wrong – 'doing the right thing'.
- How one should act in a certain situation.

Why should we bother with ethics?

Pros	Cons
• To protect the public interest	• Increased cost of sourcing materials from ethical sources
• To avoid discipline/fines	
• Improved reputation	• Lose profit by not trading with unethical customers/suppliers
• Good ethics can attract customers	
• Good ethics can result in a more effective workforce	• Waste of management time?
• Ethics can give cost savings	
• Ethics can reduce risk	

Fundamental principles

Professional Competence and Due Care	The necessary professional knowledge and skills required to carry out work should be present.
Objectivity	Business or professional judgement is not compromised because of bias or conflict of interest.
Professional Behaviour	All relevant laws and regulations must be complied with and any actions that would bring the profession into disrepute avoided.
Integrity	This implies fair dealing and truthfulness.
Confidentiality	Information obtained in a business relationship is not to be disclosed to third parties without specific authority being given to do so, unless there is a legal or professional reason to do so.

Examples

Accounting issues	Creative accounting.
	Directors' pay.
	Bribes.
	Insider trading.
Production	Should the company produce certain products at all, e.g. tobacco.
	Should the company be concerned about the effects on the environment of its production processes?
	Should the company test its products on animals?
Sales / marketing	Price fixing and anticompetitive behaviour.
	Is it ethical to target advertising at children?
	Should products be advertised by junk mail or spam email?
Personnel	Discrimination.
	The contract of employment must offer a fair balance of power between employee and employer.
	The workplace must be a safe and healthy place to operate in.

Safeguards

Business organisations can create a culture that makes it as easy as possible for employees to follow their professional codes and behave ethically.

Six values that organisations can apply in order to accomplish this can be remembered using the acronym HOTTER.

Honesty	Employees should be encouraged to be honest at all times.
Openness	The organisation should be willing to freely provide information (as needed) to stakeholders.
Transparency	The organisation makes it easy for key stakeholders to review its activities.
Trust	Organisations need to be trustworthy in their dealings with others and attempt to work in the best interests of as many stakeholders as possible.
Empowerment	Giving employees and other stakeholders more ability to make their own decisions.
Respect	All employees and stakeholders should be treated with dignity by the organisation regardless of their age, gender, ethnicity, religion or sexuality.

Sustainability

What do we mean by 'sustainability'?

- Sustainable development is development that meets the needs of the **present** without compromising the ability of **future** generations to meet their own needs.

  (The UN's Bruntland Report).

- A sustainable business is a business that offers products and services that fulfil society's needs while placing an equal emphasis on **people**, **planet** and **profits**.

  (The Sustainable Business Network)

Examples of unsustainable practices

Economic

- Underpayment of taxes – not contributing to maintaining the country's infrastructure (schools, roads, etc.).
- Bribery and corruption.

Social

- Rich companies exploiting labour in developing countries as cheap manufacturing.

Environmental

- Long term damage to the environment from carbon dioxide and other greenhouse gases.

Benefits of acting sustainably

- Potential cost savings – e.g. due to lower energy usage.
- Avoiding fines – e.g. for pollution.
- Short term gain in sales – e.g. if customers are influenced by sustainability related labels on products.
- Long term gain in sales – e.g. due to enhanced PR and reputation.
- Better risk management – e.g. pre-empting changes in regulations.
- Sustainability is one aspects of a firm's commitment to CSR.

Sustainability and the accounting system

The Accountancy Department

- The paperless office – how much of the paper used in the accounting department is justified?
- Emailing invoices to customers rather than posting paper versions.
- Emailing statements to customers rather than posting paper versions.
- The energy usage for lights, the machines and for heating.
- The use of sustainable materials for the office furniture.
- The level of carbon dioxide produced (if any).

'What gets measured gets done'

- The accountancy function can help champion sustainability by suggesting environmental performance measures and measuring these KPIs.

Index